THE POWER OF THE SPOKEN WORD

Paperback: 978-819596173-3

Printed by:

Sanage Publishing House LLP
Mumbai, India

sanagepublishing@gmail.com

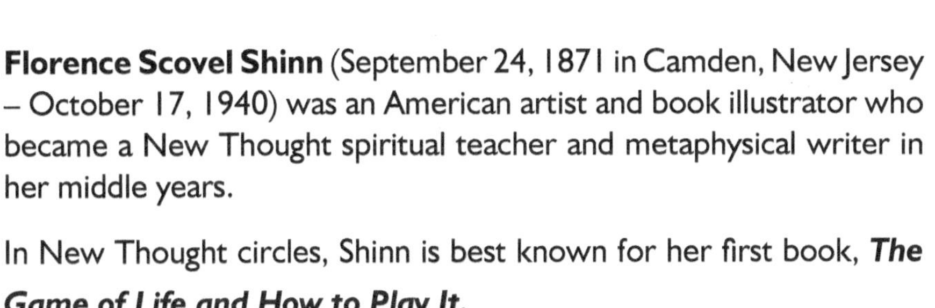

Florence Scovel Shinn (September 24, 1871 in Camden, New Jersey – October 17, 1940) was an American artist and book illustrator who became a New Thought spiritual teacher and metaphysical writer in her middle years.

In New Thought circles, Shinn is best known for her first book, ***The Game of Life and How to Play It.***

CONTENTS

FOREWORD

Florence Scovel Shinn taught metaphysics in New York for many years. Her meetings were well attended and in that way she was the means of bringing the message to a considerable number of people.

Her books have had a wide circulation not only in America but abroad. They seem to have a knack of finding their way to remote and unexpected places in Europe and other parts of the world. Now and again we meet someone who came into Truth through finding a Florence Shinn book in the most improbable location.

One secret of her success was that she was always herself . . . colloquial, informal, friendly, and humorous. She never sought to be literary, conventional, or impressive. For this reason she appealed to thousands who would not have taken the spiritual message through the more conservative and dignified forms, or have been willing to read . . . at least in the beginning . . . the standard metaphysical books.

She herself was very spiritual, although this was usually hidden behind a matter of fact and carefree treatment of her subject. The technical or academic approach was not for her. She taught by familiar, practical, and everyday examples.

She had been by profession an artist and book illustrator before becoming a Truth teacher, and belonged to an old Philadelphia family.

She left a collection of notes and memoranda which have been made into the present book. May it have a wide circulation.

~ Emmet Fox

CHAPTER 1.
Weapons Ye Know Not Of

"I have weapons ye know not of! I have ways ye know not of! I have channels ye know not of! Mysterious weapons, mysterious ways, mysterious channels! For God works in mysterious ways His wonders to perform." The trouble with most people is that they want to know the way and the channels beforehand. They want to tell Supreme Intelligence just how their prayers should be answered. They do not trust the wisdom and ingenuity of God. They pray, giving Infinite Intelligence definite directions how to work, thereby limiting the Holy One of Israel.

Jesus Christ said: "When ye pray, believe ye have it." What could be more simple or direct? "Become as a little child if you would enter the kingdom." We might paraphrase the scriptures and say, have the expectancy of a little child and your prayers will be answered. A child waits with joyful expectancy for his toys at Christmas. I give the illustration of the little boy who asked for a drum for Christmas. The child does not lie awake at night agonizing over his drum wondering whether he will get it. He goes to bed and sleeps like a top. He jumps out of bed in the morning ready for the happy day before him. He looks with wonder at that which is before him.

The grown-up person spends sleepless nights agonizing over his problem. Instead of a drum, he has spoken for a large sum of money.

He can't think of any way it can come, and will it come on time? He will tell you he has perfect faith in God, but he would like to know more about the channel and how it is to be done. The answer comes, "I have weapons ye know not of." "My ways are ingenious; my methods are sure."

"Trust in me, commit your ways unto me." Committing your ways unto the Lord seems very difficult to most people. It means, of course, to follow intuition, for intuition is the magic path, the beeline to your demonstration. Intuition is a Spiritual faculty above the intellect. It is the "still small voice" commonly called a hunch, which says, "This is the way, walk ye in it." I refer to intuition very often for it is the most important part of Spiritual development. It is Divine Guidance. It is the God within, it is the eye which watches over Israel and never slumbers or sleeps. With it, nothing is unimportant. Acknowledge me in all your ways and I will make plain your path. Remember despise not the day of small things (of seemingly unimportant events).

It is very difficult for a person who has always followed the reasoning mind, to suddenly follow intuition, especially people who have, what they call, regular habits. They are accustomed to doing the same thing every day at the same time.

Meals like clockwork. They get up at a certain time and go to bed at a certain time. Any deviation upsets them.

We have the power of choice, we may follow the magic path of intuition, or the long and hard road of experience, by following the reasoning mind. By following the superconscious we attain the heights. In the intuition, are the pictures of eternal youth and eternal life, where death itself is overcome. We have the power to impress the subconscious mind with the picture of Eternal youth and Eternal life. The subconscious, being simply power without direction, carries out the idea, and we have our bodies transmuted into the body which can never die. We see this idea partly expressed in the moving picture

"The Lost Horizon." Shangrila was a symbolic picture of the "World of the Wondrous," where all conditions are perfect.

There is a Spiritual prototype of your body and affairs. I call it the Divine Design and this Divine Design is a Perfect Idea in your superconscious mind. Most people are far from expressing the Divine Idea of their bodies and affairs. They have stamped the contrary pictures of disease, old age, and death upon the subconscious, and it has carefully carried out their orders. Now we must give a new order; "Let me now express the Divine Idea in my mind, body and affairs." If you will impress the subconscious by repeating this statement, you will be amazed at the changes which soon take place. You will be bombarded by new ideas and new ideals. A chemical change will take place in your body. Your environment will change for the better, for you are expanding rapidly into the Divine Plan, where all conditions are permanently perfect.

"Lift up your heads, ye gates, and be ye lifted up, ye everlasting doors; and the King of Glory shall come in. Who is this King of Glory? The Lord (or Law) strong and mighty. The Lord mighty in battle."

Now remember, the Bible is talking about thoughts and states of consciousness. Here is a picture of the Perfect Ideas of the superconscious mind, rushing into your conscious mind. Gates and doors are lifted up, and "The King of Glory comes in." "Who is this King of Glory? The Lord strong and mighty. The Lord mighty in battle." This King of Glory has weapons ye know not of and puts to fight the army of the aliens (the negative thoughts entrenched in your consciousness for countless ages). These negative thoughts have always defeated the manifestation of your heart's desire. They are the thought forms which you have built up in your subconscious by constantly thinking the same thoughts. You have built up a fixed idea that "Life is hard and filled with disappointments." You will meet these thoughts as concrete experiences in life, for "Out of the imaginations of the heart come the issues of life."

"My ways are ways of pleasantness." We should all build up in consciousness a picture of peace, harmony and beauty and some day it will push itself into visibility. The Divine Idea of your life often flashes across your consciousness as something too good to be true. Very few people fulfill their destinies. Destiny means the place you were destined to fill. We are fully equipped for the Divine Plan of our lives. We are more than equal to every situation. If we could get the realization back of these words' doors would fly open and channels be cleared. We could actually hear the hum of Divine activity, for we would be linked with Infinite Intelligence which knows no defeat. Opportunities would come to us from unexpected quarters. Divine activity would operate in and through all our affairs and the Divine Idea would come to pass.

God is Love but God is Law, "If ye love me, keep my commandments" (or laws). Dr. Ernest Wilson told me that his first knowledge of Truth came through reading Emerson's "Concentration." Concentration means loving absorption. We see children lovingly absorbed in their play. We can only be a success in a line which interests us greatly. Great inventors are never bored with their work, or they would not bring forth great inventions. Never try to force a child to be something he does not want to be. He will only prove a failure. The first start toward success is to be glad you are yourself. So many people are bored by themselves. They have no self-reliance and are always wishing they were someone else.

When I was in London, I saw a man on the street selling a new song, it was called, "I'm tickled to death I'm me." I thought that was a wonderful idea start out by being glad you are yourself. Then you can expand rapidly into the Divine plan of your life where you fulfill your destiny. You may be sure that the Divine plan of your life will give you perfect satisfaction. You will no longer envy anyone. People often become impatient and discouraged. I was inspired by reading in the paper about Omaha, the famous racehorse. The article said, "Omaha has to run a mile before he gets into his stride." There are, no doubt, a lot of Omahas in the world, but they can get into their Spiritual stride, and win the race, in the twinkling of an eye.

"Delight thyself also in the Lord, and He shall give thee the desires of thine heart." Delight thyself in the law and it will give to thee the desires of thine heart. "Delighting yourself in the law" means to enjoy making a demonstration. To enjoy trusting God, means to be happy in following your intuitive leads. Most people say, "Oh dear; I've got to demonstrate money again;" or "Oh dear, my hunches make me so nervous, I haven't the nerve to follow them." People enjoy playing golf and tennis, why can't we enjoy playing the game of life? It is because we are playing with unseen forces. With golf or tennis, they have balls they can see and a goal which is visible to the naked eye; but how much more important is this game of life? The goal is the Divine plan of your life where all conditions are permanently perfect.

"In all thy ways acknowledge Him and He will make plain thy paths." Every moment we can link with intuition, will give us as definite a lead as a signpost. So many people are leading such complicated lives because they are trying to think things out instead of "intuiting" the way out.

I know a woman who says she has a thorough knowledge of Truth and its application but the minute she has a problem she reasons and weights and measures the situation. It is never solved. Intuition flies out of the window when reason comes to the door. Intuition is a Spiritual faculty, the superconscious, and never explains itself. There came a voice before me, saying, "This is the way, walk ye in it." Someone asked me if the reasoning mind was ever any good. The reasoning mind must be redeemed. Trust in Spiritual law and "it will be given you."

Your part is to be a good receiver, prepare for your blessing, rejoice, and give thanks and it will come to pass.

I have weapons ye know not of, I have ways which will astound you.

CHAPTER 2.
I Give Unto You Power

God's gift to man is power; power and dominion over all created things; his mind, his body, and affairs. All unhappiness comes from lack of power. Man imagines himself weak and the victim of circumstances, claiming that "Conditions over which he had no control" caused his defeat. Man by himself, is indeed, a victim of circumstances; but linked with God-power all things are possible.

Through a knowledge of metaphysics, we are discovering how this can be done. By your word you contact this power. Then, miraculously, every burden is lifted, and every battle is won. Life and death are in the power of the tongue. Watch your words with all diligence. You are continually reaping the fruits of your words. And he that overcometh and keepeth my works to the end, to him will I give power and dominion over the nations." Overcoming means to conquer all doubts, fears, and negative vibrations. One man with perfect peace and perfect poise, filled with love and good-will, could dissolve all negative vibrations. They would melt away like snow under the sun. Jesus Christ said: "All power is given unto me to bring heaven upon earth." Let us give thanks that this is now coming to pass for evil is unreal and leaves no stain. This God- power is within you, your superconscious mind. It is the realm of inspiration, revelation, and illumination. It is the realm of miracles and wonders. Quick and seemingly impossible changes take place for your good. A door opens where there were no doors. Supply appears from hidden and unexpected channels, for "God has weapons ye know not of."

To work with God-power you must give it right of way and still the reasoning mind. The instant you ask, Infinite Intelligence knows the way of fulfillment. Man's part is to rejoice and give thanks and act his Faith. A very well-known woman in England told of this experience: She was asking, with great feeling, for a realization of God. These words came to her "Act as though I were, and I am." It is exactly what I say, over and over again only active faith impresses the subconscious, and unless you impress the subconscious, there are no results.

I will now give you an example to show you just how the law works. A woman came to me whose heart's desire was her right marriage and happy home. She was very fond of a certain man, but he was a most difficult person. After having shown her every attention and devotion, he suddenly changed, and dropped out of her life. She was unhappy, resentful, and discouraged. I said, "Now this is the time to prepare for your happy home! Buy little things for it as if you hadn't a minute to spare." She became quite interested in shopping for her happy home, when all appearances were against it. "Now," I said, "you'll have to perfect yourself on the situation and become immune to all resentment and unhappiness." I gave her the statement: "I am now immune to all hurt and resentment: my poise is built upon a rock, the Christ within." I said, "When you are immune to all hurt and resentment, this man will be given you or his equivalent." It took many months, when one evening she came to see me and said, "I have only the kindest and most friendly feelings for this man. If he isn't the Divine selection, I would be happy without him."

Not long after, she happened to meet the man. He was so sorry for the way he had acted. He begged her to forgive him. Not long after, they were married, and a happy home came into manifestation. It had built itself around her active Faith.

Your only enemies are within yourself. The woman's enemies were "hurt" and "resentment." They are indeed "serpents and scorpions." Many lives have been wrecked by these two enemies. Linked with God-power, all opposition vanished from this woman's life. Nothing could by any means hurt her.

Think what that means, to have a life free from all unhappy experiences. It is done through making a conscious contact with God-power every instant.

Many times, in the Bible, the word "power" is mentioned. "Thou shalt remember the Lord thy God, for it is He that giveth thee power to get wealth."

A person with a rich consciousness attracts riches. A person with a poor consciousness attracts poverty. I have seen people in this Truth, rise out of lack and limitation by linking with the God-power within, not depending on the external, trusting in God gives you irresistible power, for this Supreme Intelligence only, knows the Way of fulfillment. "Trust in Me and I will bring it to pass."

All our knowledge of Truth can bring us is to know that God is the only Power. One Power, one Presence, one Plan. When you have the fixed idea that there is only one Power in the universe, God- power, all appearance of evil will disappear from your world. In getting a demonstration we must acknowledge only one Power. Evil comes from man's own "vain imaginings." Withdraw all power from evil and it is powerless to hurt.

I will give you an example which shows the working of the law. I was in a restaurant with a friend who spilled something on her dress. She was sure it would leave a stain. I said, "We'll give it a treatment." I made the statement, "Evil is unreal and leaves no stain." I said, "Now, don't look, leave it to Infinite Intelligence." In about an hour we took a look and there was not the slightest stain.

What is true of a little thing is true of a big thing. You can use this statement for past misfortunes or mistakes, and somehow or other, under Grace, the effects will disappear, they will leave no stain.

Many people are using personal-power instead of God-power, which always brings unhappy reaction. Personal-power means forcing personal will. I will give the example of a woman I knew a long time ago. She married a man who worked on a newspaper drawing a comic strip. His drawings demanded a knowledge of slang, which he used on every occasion. She decided he should cultivate his mind and read the classics. They moved to a college town so that he could go to college. She insisted upon his going to college. He resisted a little at first then he grew to like it! Soon he was steeped in the classics. He wouldn't talk anything but Plato and Aristotle. He wanted the food cooked the way they cooked and eat the simple food they ate. Her life had become a nightmare. After that, she never tried to change people. The only person to change, is yourself. As you change, all the conditions around you will change! People will change!

When you are undisturbed by a situation it falls away of its own weight. Your life is out-pictured by the sum total of your subconscious beliefs. Wherever you go, you take these conditions with you.

"I am strong in the Lord and the Power of His might."

"I am backed by unnumbered hosts of power." Power means dominion and dominion means control. Man, controls conditions by a knowledge of Spiritual law. Suppose your problem is lack or limitation. Your urgent need is supply. Link with this God-power within and give thanks for your immediate supply. If you are too close to the situation, if you are filled with doubts and fears, go to a Practitioner for help, someone to see clearly for you.

A man told me while at a Truth Centre at Pittsburgh he heard people talking about me and he said, "Who in heck is Florence Scovel Shinn?" Someone replied, "Oh, she wrote The Game of Life, if you write to her, she'll get you a miracle." He said he promptly wrote to me and got a demonstration. Jesus Christ said, "When two of you agree, it shall be done." Do not hesitate to ask for help if you cannot see clearly your good. Jesus Christ saw clearly for the people he healed. He did not tell them to heal themselves. Of course, you can reach the state where you do not need any help, when you have the fixed idea that God's Power is the only Power and that God's Plan is the only Plan.

We cannot take blessings from Infinite Intelligence; they must be given us. Man's part is to be a grateful receiver. "Behold I give unto you power to tread on serpents and scorpions and over all the power of the enemy, and nothing shall by any means hurt you." "Thou madest him to have dominion over the works of thy hands and hath put all things under his feet. All sheep and oxen, yea and the beasts of the fields." This is God's idea of man, but man's idea of himself is one of limitation and failure. It is only in a big moment, that man seems to rise to his power and dominion.

It isn't until we face a situation of lack, that we suddenly express the power which has already been given us. I have known people who are usually nervous and anxious to become poised and powerful when confronted by a big situation.

"Hear, Oh! Israel! Ye have no need to fight, stand ye still and see the salvation of the Lord." People often ask, "What does it mean to stand still, to do nothing at all?" "Standing still" means to keep your poise. I said to a man who was tense and anxious, "Take it easy and see the salvation of the Lord." He replied, "My; that has helped me a lot." Most people are trying too hard. They carry their burdens and fight their battles and are, therefore, always in a turmoil and never get, what we call, a demonstration. Stand aside and see the salvation of the Lord. We might paraphrase the Scriptures and say, "Hear! O! Israel, you will never win this battle by fighting leave it entirely to Me, and it will be given you."

Following the magic path of intuition, you escape all complications and friction, and make a beeline to your demonstration. Remember we are told not to despise the day of small things. It is a great mistake to think that anything is unimportant. I was going to a shop to buy two articles. In my vicinity are two shops, an expensive one and one where all the things are a little cheaper, but the articles are exactly the same. The reasoning mind said, "Go to the cheaper place" but intuition said, "Go to the expensive place." Of course, I followed that magic path. I told the clerk what I wanted. He said: "The two articles are today sold for the price of one, because they are advertising one of the products." So, intuition led me to the right place and price. The difference in price was only about fifty cents but intuition always looks after our interests. If I had been trying to get something cheap, I would have gone to the other shop and paid twice as much. Learn from the little things, and you will be ready to handle the big things.

Studying closely the Scriptures, we find, God's gift to man is

power. The things and conditions automatically follow. God gives manpower to get well. He gives manpower over the elements. He gives manpower to heal sickness, and to cast out devils.

"They that wait upon the Lord shall renew their strength. They shall mount up with wings and eagles, they shall run and not be weary, and shall walk and not faint."

Let us realize that this invincible power is within reach of all. "Whosoever calleth on the name of the Lord, shall be delivered!" So, we find the Word links man with omnipotence. This Supreme Intelligence is more than equal to lifting every burden and fighting every battle.

All power is given unto me to bring my heaven upon my earth.

CHAPTER 3.
Be Strong; Fear Not

Be strong! Fear not; Fear is man's only adversary. You face defeat whenever you are fearful! Fear of lack! Fear of failure! Fear of loss! Fear of personality! Fear of criticism! Fear robs you of all power, for you have lost your contact with the Universal Powerhouse. "Why are ye fearful, Oh ye of little faith?" Fear is inverted faith. It is faith turned upside down. When you are fearful you begin to attract the thing, you fear you are magnetizing it. You are hypnotized by the race thought when you are afraid.

Daniel was undisturbed because he knew his God was stronger than the lions, His God made the lions as harmless as kittens, so walk up to your lion as quickly as possible and see for yourself. Perhaps, all your life you've been running away from some particular lion. It has made your life miserable and your hair grey. A hairdresser once told me that she knew a woman, whose grey hair returned to its natural color when she stopped worry. A woman said to me during an interview, "I'm not a bit fearful, but I worry a lot." Fear and worry are twins and are the same thing. If you were fearless your worry cells would be dried up. Why are ye worried, Oh ye of little faith? I think the most prevalent fear is the fear of loss. Perhaps you have everything that life can give, but in creeps the old lion of apprehension. You hear him growling, "It's too good to be true! It can't last." If he gets your attention, you may well worry.

Many people have lost what they prized most dearly in life. That is because invariably they fear loss. The only weapon you can use against your lions is your word. Your word is your wand, filled with magic and power. You wave your wand over your lion and transmute him into a kitten. BUT the lion will remain a lion unless you walk up to him. You may well ask, "HOW do we walk up to lions?" Moses said unto his people, "Fear ye not, stand still and see the salvation of the Lord, which He will show to you this day for the Egyptians whom ye have seen today, ye shall see them again, no more forever! The Lord shall fight for you, and ye shall hold your peace." What a marvelous arrangement! Infinite Intelligence knows the way out. Infinite Intelligence knows where the supply is, for every demand. But we must trust It, keep our poise, and give It right of way. So many people are afraid of other people. They run away from disagreeable situations, so of course, the situation runs after them.

"The Lord is my light and my salvation: whom shall, I fear? The Lord is the strength of my life: of whom shall I be afraid?" The twenty- seventh Psalm is one of the most triumphant Psalms! It is also rhythmic and musical. The writer realized that no enemy could harm him, for the Lord was his light and his salvation. Now remember, your only enemies are within yourself. The Bible is speaking of the enemy thoughts, your doubts, fears, hates, resentments, and forebodings. Every negative situation in your life is a crystallized thought, it has been built up out of your own vain imaginings! But these situations cannot stand the light of truth. So, you face the situation fearlessly, saying, "The Lord is my light and salvation; whom shall I fear?" Jesus Christ was the greatest of metaphysicians and gave us definite rules for controlling conditions through word and thought. "Thou hast made me wiser than mine enemies." First of all, you must be wiser than your enemy thoughts, the army of the aliens. You must answer every negative thought with a word of authority. The army of the aliens will chant: "Business is dull and money is scarce." Immediately you reply, "My supply comes from God and now appears like mushrooms overnight." There are no hard times in the kingdom. You may have to keep this up for quite a while, like the song of the katydids "Katy did, Katy didn't." and so on. Finally, you win out, for the truth must prevail and you have put to flight, the army of the aliens. Then, when you are off your guard, the army of the aliens begins again; "You're not appreciated, you'll never be a success." You answer immediately: "God appreciates me, therefore man appreciates me. Nothing can interfere with my divinely designed success." Finally, the army of the aliens is dissolved and dissipated, because you do not give it your attention. You have starved the aliens out. Starve out the fear thoughts by not giving them your attention and acting your faith. The lion draws his fierceness from your fear, his roar is in the tremors of your heart. Stand still like Daniel, and you too shall hear the rush of angels sent to take your part.

The mission of Jesus Christ was to wake people up. "Awake thou that sleepeth." People were asleep in the Adamic dream of opposites. Lack, loss, failure, sin, sickness, and death seemed realities to them. The story of Adam is, that he ate of the tree of Illusion and fell into a deep sleep. In this deep sleep he vainly imagined good and evil.

Bernard Shaw, in his book Back to Methuselah, says: "Adam invented murder, birth and death and all negative conditions." It was the development of the reasoning mind. Of course, Adam stands for Generic Mind. In the Garden of Eden stage, man functioned only in the superconscious. Whatever he desired or required was always at hand. With the development of the reasoning mind came the fall of man. He reasoned himself into lack, limitations, and failure. He earned his bread by the sweat of the brow, instead of being Divinely provided for.

Jesus Christ's message was to bring people back into the "fourth dimension," the Garden of Eden consciousness. In the 14th Chapter of John, we find the summing up of all His teachings. He called it, "The

Gospel," which means "Good Tidings."

With amazing simplicity and directness, He told the people that if they asked, believing, they would receive attributing the power always to the Father within. God is the Giver, man the receiver! This Supreme Intelligence supplies man with all that he desires or requires! This was certainly a doctrine to wake people up! He proved His statements with miracles and wonders. One of the most dramatic miracles was the healing of the man who had been blind from birth. The opponents of Jesus questioned the man, hoping to find something against Him. But the man would only say: "One thing I know; whereas I was blind, now I can see." This is a marvelous statement to make to yourself. "Whereas I was blind, now I can see." Perhaps you were blind to your good, blind to your opportunities, blind to your intuitive leads, blind to appearances, mistaking friends for enemies. When you are awake to your good, you know there are no enemies, for God utilizes every person and situation for your good. Hindrances are friendly and obstacles steppingstones. One with God, you become invincible. This is a very powerful statement: "God's Invincible Power sweeps all before it. I ride the waves into my Promised Land." Riding the waves, they take you to your destination, free from the undertow of negative thinking, which would pull you down. Your thoughts and desires are always taking you somewhere. Prentice Mulford says: "The persistent purpose, that strong desire, that never ceasing longing, is a seed in the mind. It is rooted there, it is alive! It never stops growing!

There is a wonderful law involved in it. This law when known, followed out and trusted, leads every individual to mighty and beautiful results. The law followed with our eyes open, leads to more and more happiness in life; but followed blindly with our eyes shut, leads to misery!"

This means that desire is a tremendous vibratory force and must be rightly directed. Take this statement: "I only desire that which Infinite Intelligence desires through me. I claim that which is mine by Divine right, and under Grace in a Perfect Way!" You will then cease desiring the wrong things, and the right desires will take their place. Your dreary desires are answered drearily, your impatient desires are long delayed or violently fulfilled. It is important never to lose sight of this. Many unhappy situations have been brought about through dreary or impatient desires.

I will give an example of a woman who was married to a man who wanted her to go somewhere with him every evening. It wore her out and night after night she wished impatiently that she could stay at home and read a book. The desire was so strong it commenced to bud. Her husband went off with another woman. She lost him and his support, but she had the time to stay at home and read a book. Nothing has ever come uninvited into your life.

Prentice Mulford has also some interesting ideas on work. He said: "To succeed in any undertaking, any art or any trade or any profession, simply keep it ever persistently fixed in mind as an aim, and then study to make all effort toward it play or recreation. The moment it becomes hard work, we are not advancing."

As I look back on my experiences in the art world, I see how true this is. From the Academy of Fine Arts in Philadelphia, came eight men, all of about the same age, who became distinguished and successful artists. They were called "The Eight" in Contemporary Art. Not one of them was ever known to work hard. They never drew from the antique; they never did anything in an academic way. They simply expressed themselves. They painted and drew because they loved it - for the fun of it. They tell an amusing story of one of them who became a very well-known landscape artist, taking many medals and honorary mentions at exhibits. He had a one-man show in New York City, at one of the big galleries, and was seated reading a paper. An enthusiastic woman rushed up to him and said: "Can you tell me anything about the wonderful man who painted these adorable pictures?" He replied: "Sure, I'm the guy that painted the damn things." He painted for fun, he didn't care whether people liked his pictures or not.

Whereas I was blind, now I can see, my right work, my perfect self-expression. Whereas I was blind, now I can see clearly and distinctly the Divine plan of my life. Whereas I was blind, now I can see, that God's power is the only power and that God's plan is the only plan. The race thought is still with a belief in insecurity. "Awake, thou that sleepeth!" God is your eternal security of mind, body, and affairs. "Let not your heart be troubled, neither be afraid." If you were wide awake to your good, you could not be troubled and fearful! Waking up to the truth, that there is no loss, lack or failure in the kingdom of reality loss, lack and failure would disappear from your life. They come from your own vain imaginings.

The following is an example, illustrating the working of the law. A number of years ago, when I was in London, I bought a wonderful fountain pen at Asprey's. It was Japanese and was called a Namike Pen. It was quite expensive, and they gave me, with it, a guarantee that it would last thirty years. I was very much impressed, because every summer, on the 5th of August, they wrote me asking how the pen was getting along; one might have thought I had bought a horse. It was no ordinary pen and was very satisfactory. I always carried it with me and one day I lost it. I immediately commenced denying loss. I said; "There is no loss in Divine Mind, therefore I cannot lose the Namike Pen. It will be restored to me or its equivalent." No shops that I knew of in New York City carried these pens and London was a long way off, but I was charged with Divine Confidence, I couldn't lose the Namike Pen. One day, going along Fifth Avenue in a bus, my eye caught a sign on a shop for the fraction of a second. It seemed to stand out in the light. It read, "Oriental Craft Shop." I had never heard of it, but I had a strong hunch to go in and ask for a Namike Pen. I got off the bus and went into the shop and asked. The saleswoman replied, "Why yes, we have quite an assortment, they have just been reduced to $2.50." I praised the Lord and gave thanks. I bought three and told the above story at one of my meetings. They were soon sold out as people rushed to get them. This was certainly an amazing working of the law, but I was wide awake to my good. I did not let any grass grow under my intuitive lead.

The Truth student knows he must prove the principle in his everyday affairs. "Acknowledge me in all your ways and I will direct your paths." "Verily, verily, I say unto you, he that believeth on me, the works that I do, he shall do also, and greater works than these, shall he do, because I go unto my father." What wonderful Faith Jesus Christ had in man! He held the vision of the race to come. The man made in God's likeness and image, (imagination). "And whatsoever ye shall ask in my name, that will I do, that the Father may be glorified in the Son." If ye shall ask anything in my name, I will do it. He explained to the people that they were under a system of gifts. God was the Giver, man the receiver. "Believest thou not that I am in the father and the father in me? The words that I speak unto you I speak not of myself but the Father that dwelleth in me He doeth the works." He told people to "seek the kingdom," the realm of perfect ideas, where all things would be added unto them. He woke them up!

"Whereas I was blind, now I can see, there is nothing to fear for there is no power to hurt. I see clearly before me the open road of fulfilment. There are no obstacles on my pathway." Thou madest Him to have dominion over the works of thy hand: thou hast put all things under His feet. Psalm 8: 6

CHAPTER 4.
The Glory Of The Lord

In the dictionary, I find the word glory, defined as radiance, splendor. "Mine eyes have seen the radiance of the Lord" that means the law in action. We cannot see God, for God is principle, Power, the Supreme Intelligence within us, but what we see are the proofs of God. "Prove Thou me herewith, saith the Lord of Hosts, if I will not open the windows of hearing, and pour you out a blessing, so great, there be not room enough to receive it." We prove God by directing God-power and trusting in It to do the work. Every time we get a demonstration, we have proved God. If you have not received the desires of the heart, you have "asked amiss," that is, you have "not prayed aright." You receive your answer in the same way in which you sent out your demand. Your dreary desires are answered drearily, your impatient desires are long delayed or violently fulfilled.

Suppose you are resenting lack and limitation and living in poor surroundings. You say with great feeling, "I want to live in a big house, with beautiful surroundings!" Sooner or later, you may find yourself a caretaker in a big and beautiful house, but you have no share in this opulence. This idea came to me as I was passing Andrew Carnegie's house and grounds on Fifth Avenue. It was all closed and the entrance and windows boarded up. There was just one window open in the basement. This is where the caretaker lived. It was certainly a dreary picture. So, ask (or wish) with praise and thanksgiving, so that you will see the glory of the law in action.

All life is vibration. You combine with what you notice, or you combine with what you vibrate to. If you are vibrating to injustice and resentment, you will meet it on your pathway, at every step. You will certainly think it is a hard world and that everybody is against you. Hermes Trismegistus said several thousand years ago, "To change your mood you must change your vibrations." I make it even stronger; I say, to change your world, you must change your vibrations. Turn on a different current in your battery of thought, and you'll see the difference immediately. Suppose you have been resenting people and saying you are not appreciated. Take the statement:

"God appreciates me, therefore, man appreciates me, I appreciate myself." Immediately you will meet with some recognition on the external.

You are now a master workman, and your tools are your words. Be sure you are building constructively, according to the Divine Plan. Judge Troward said: "Man is a distributor of God-Power, he does not create this force." We find in Hebrews: "What is man that Thou art mindful of him? And the son of man that thou visitest him? Thou madest him a little lower than the angels; and hath crowned him with glory and honor. Thou madest him to have dominion over the works of thy hands, Thou hast put all things under his feet." Thou hast put all things under our understanding.

We are now coming into an understanding age.

We no longer have the faith of peasants; we have understanding faith. Solomon said: "With all your getting, get understanding"; understanding of the working of Spiritual Law, so that we distribute this power within us in a constructive way.

The law of laws is to do unto others as you would be done by; for, whatever you send out comes back and what you do to others will be done to you. So, the woman who refrains from criticizing, saves herself from criticism. Critical people are always being criticized. They are living in that vibration. They also have rheumatism, for acid thoughts produce acid in the blood, which causes pain in the joints. I read an article in the newspaper. It said a physician had had a peculiar experience with one of his patients. The woman had boils, every time her mother-in-law paid her a visit. There is nothing peculiar in this, as she was boiling within (how many times we have heard people say they were in a boiling rage), so the boils appeared on her body. This does not include all mothers-in-law. I have known some very wonderful ones who have brought only peace and harmony with them. Skin trouble shows that someone has got under your skin. You have been irritated or angered. Here we see again that man gives direction to this God-power, through himself. Vibrative to this power, all things are under his feet. "All sheep and oxen, yea the beasts of the field. The fowl of the air and the fish of the sea, whatsoever passes through the paths of the seas." What a picture of power and dominion for man!

Man has power and dominion over the elements. We should be able "to rebuke the wind and the waves." We should be able to put an end to drought. I read in the paper that the people in a certain drought district were requested not to sing, "It ain't going to rain no more." Knowing something of metaphysics, they realized the power of negative words. They felt it had something to do with the drought. We should be able to stop floods and epidemics, "For man is given power and dominion over all created things." Every time we get a demonstration, we are proving our power and dominion.

We must be lifted up in consciousness for the King of Glory to come in! As we read the statement: "If thine eye be single, thy whole body shall be full of light," we seem flooded with an inner radiance. The single eye means to see good only, to be undisturbed by appearances of evil. As Jesus Christ said: "Judge not by appearances: judge righteous (right) judgment." There is an occult law of indifference. Jesus Christ knew this law. "None of these things move me." None of these things disturb me, we might say in our modern language. Selfishness and personal will bring defeat and failure. "Unless the Lord builds the house, they labor in vain who build it." The imaging faculty is a creative faculty, and your fear-pictures will appear on the external, the result of your own distorted imagination. With the single eye, man sees only the Truth. He sees through evil, knowing out of it comes good. He transmutes injustice into justice and disarms his seeming enemies by sending good will. He is now backed by unnumbered hosts of Power, for the single eye sees only victory.

We read in mythology of the Cyclops, a race of giants said to have inhabited Sicily. These giants had only one eye in the middle of the forehead. The seat of the imaging faculty is situated in the forehead (between the eyes), so these fabled giants came from this idea. You are indeed a giant when you have "the single eye."

Jesus Christ, the greatest of all teachers, reiterated, "Now is the appointed time, Today is the day of your salvation." A few days ago, I saw a motion picture which showed the futility of trying to live in or bring back the past. It is a French picture and is called "Life Dances On." It is the story of a woman, who, when sixteen, had gone to her first ball. She is now a widow of about thirty-five. She had married for money and had never known happiness. When burning old papers, she came across a faded dance programme. On it were the names of six men she had danced with at the ball. Each had sworn to love her all his life! As she sits with the programme in her hands the memory of the ball is pictured on the screen, a scene of loveliness, the dancers almost floating to the strains of an entrancing waltz. Her life is now empty, and she decides to recover her lost youth, by finding out what had become of the men whose names were on the programme. A friend who is with her says, "You cannot recapture your lost youth; if you go back, you lose the things of today." However, she goes in search of them, and with all, comes disillusion. One did not remember her at all. When she said: "Don't you remember me? I am Christine!" He replied, "Christine who?" Some of them were living sordid lives. At last, she returns to the town of her girlhood, where the fifth man lived. He had become a hairdresser. He talks to her gaily of old times, while he gives her a permanent wave. He says, "I don't suppose you remember your first ball, it was right here in this town, and tonight there will be a dance in the same place. Do come with me, it will remind you of the old days!" She goes to the ball; everything looks cheap and tawdry. Unattractive, badly dressed people are on the dance floor. She requests the orchestra to play her waltz, the waltz of her lost youth! Her escort tells her the others won't like such an old-fashioned waltz. However, they play it. The contrast is too much; all her illusions have vanished. She realizes the ball she remembers never really existed the way she thought it did. It was only an illusion of the past. She could not recapture her past.

It has been said that the two robbers on the Cross stood for the robbers of time. One spoke of the past and one of the futures, and Jesus Christ replied, "NOW is the appointed time, today thou shalt be with me in Paradise." In the old Sanskrit poem, we are told: "Look well, therefore, to this day. Such is the salutation of the dawn." All worry and fear are robbers of time.

The occult law underlying indifference is one of the most profound, for it contains the attainment of a state of consciousness in which the outer world of sensation has no influence upon the action of the mind, and it can, therefore, be in complete atonement with the Divine Mind. Most people's lives are a succession of disturbances: lack, loss, limitation, mothers-in-law, landlords, debt, or injustice. This world was popularly known as a "vale of tears." People were all mixed up in their own affairs, fighting their battles and carrying their burdens. If a man judges by appearances, he finds himself in an arena most of the time. The arena of adverse conditions and facing lions of lack and limitation. "If thine eye be evil (if you are imaging adverse conditions) thy whole body shall be full of darkness. If, therefore, the light that is in thee be darkness, how great is that darkness!" The light of the body is the inner eye (or imaging faculty); if, therefore, thine eye be single, you are seeing only one power, one plan and one planner, your body and affairs will be full of Light. See yourself, daily, bathed in the Light of the Christ. This inner radiance is invincible power and dissolves anything not Divinely planned. It dissolves all appearance of disease, lack, loss, or limitation. It dissolves adverse conditions, or "any weapon that is formed against you."

We have always at our command, this Light when your eye is single. We should learn to turn on this Light, with the same assurance with which we turn on the electric light. "Seek ye first the kingdom of God and His righteousness and all right things shall be added unto you." The Chinese Proverb says: "The philosopher leaves the cuff of his coat to the tailor." So, leave the plan of your life to the Divine Planner and you will find all conditions permanently perfect.

CHAPTER 5.
Peace And Prosperity

Peace be within thy walls and Prosperity within thy Palaces." In this statement from the 122nd Psalm we find that peace and prosperity go hand in hand. People who are manifesting the appearance of lack are in a state of fear and confusion. They are not wide-awake to their good and miss leads and opportunities. A peaceful person is a wide-awake person. He sees clearly and acts quickly. He never misses a trick.

I have seen people discordant and unhappy changed completely. I will give an example in order to prove the working of the law. A woman came to me in a state of abject sorrow. She looked the part. Her eyes were blurred from constant weeping. Her face was haggard and drawn. The man she loved had left her and she was certainly the most demagnetized creature I had ever seen. I noticed the shape of her face large eyes, far apart and a pointed chin. For many years I was an artist and have got into the habit of looking at people from an artist's standpoint. As I looked at this forlorn creature, I thought, her face has the modeling of a Botticelli. I often see Rembrandts, Sir Joshua Reynolds, etc., in people I meet. I spoke the Word for this woman and gave her my book, The Game of Life and How to Play It. A week or two afterwards, in walked a very dashing person. Her eyes were beautiful, and she was very pretty. I thought, her face has the modeling of a Botticelli. Suddenly I realized it was the same woman! She was happy and carefree! What had happened? Our talk and the book had brought her peace.

"Peace be within your walls!" Your "walls" are your consciousness. Jesus Christ emphasized peace and rest. "Come to me all ye that are weary and heavy laden, and I will give you rest." He was speaking of the Christ within, your superconscious mind, where there are no burdens and no battles. The doubts and fears and negative pictures are in the subconscious. When I was returning from California some years ago, I came in an aero plane. In the high altitudes I had a queer detached feeling. In that high altitude we are at peace with ourselves and with the whole world. In the high altitudes the fields are always white with the harvest. Only the emotions keep you from reaping your harvest of success, happiness, and abundance. We read in the Bible "I will restore to you the years the locusts have eaten." We might well paraphrase it and say, "I will restore to you the years the emotions have ruined." People are rocked with doubts and fears, bringing failure, unhappiness, and disease.

I read in a daily paper that the laws of the mind are being generally recognized and understood. It has been found that the fear of failure is the greatest of all fears, and at least seventy-five per cent of those examined psychologically have this failure fear. Of course, this may refer to failure of health, failure in business, finances, love, success, etc. Other important fears are fear of the dark, fear of being alone, fear of animals. Some people fear they will be misunderstood, while others fear they are losing mental control. Constant and continued fear affects the glands interferes with digestion and is usually associated with distressing nervous symptoms. It robs the body of health and destroys happiness.

Fear is man's worst enemy for you attract what you fear. It is Faith turned upside down. It is really Faith in evil instead of good. "Why are ye fearful! Oh! Ye of little faith?" The fearless, unfettered mind attracts to itself all good. Whatever you desire or require is already on your pathway. "Before ye call I have answered."

Suppose we paraphrase the Scriptures and say: "Whatever you desire or require is already planted on your pathway." Often a new word will give you sudden realization. If you are in need of any information, it will be given you. A friend told me of this surprising working of the law. She was translating an old Italian manuscript on the life of an early Persian ruler. No books in English had been written on the subject. She wondered why the publishers were holding back its publication. One evening she was eating her dinner at the Automat. She fell into a conversation with a man at the same table. She told him of the work she was doing and of the translation of the early Italian manuscript. He suddenly volunteered the information; "You'll have a hard time getting it published because this Persian ruler's ideas conflict with the ideas of the present government." He was a student and scholar and knew more than she did on the subject. Her question was answered and at the Automat. Such information could, usually, be gleaned only in the archives of some public library. God works in unexpected places His wonders to perform. She had worried about it, but when she was peaceful and happy and unconcerned, the information sailed in over a calm sea.

"Our feet shall stand within thy gates, 0 Jerusalem." Jerusalem stands for peace and the feet for understanding. So, understanding always brings us within the gates of peace. How can a person attain peace when his whole life is in a turmoil? By taking an affirmation. You cannot control your thought, but you can control your words, and eventually the word wins out. Most people have attracted inharmonious conditions because they have been fighting their battles and carrying their burdens. We must learn to get out of God's way so that He can harmonize or adjust the situation. The word "harmonize" is a very good one, for I have seen crooked places made straight, and adjustments made, that no human mind could have thought of. All that the Kingdom affords is yours, if you will give Infinite Intelligence right of way, for it has already supplied a lavish supply for every demand. But it must be fully trusted. If you doubt or fear, you lose your contact with this Supreme Force. So, if you are filled with doubts and fears, it is necessary to do something to show your faith. "Faith without works (or action) is dead." Active Faith impresses the subconscious with expectancy, and you keep your contact with Universal Intelligence. Just as Wall Street watches the market, we must watch our Faith market. Often the Faith market is down. Sometimes it goes down and down until a crash comes: some unhappy situation which we could have prevented.

We realize we followed reason instead of intuition.

A woman told me how she had several definite leads not to follow a certain course. In spite of this she followed the reasoning mind and great unhappiness developed from it. Intuition is our unerring guide. Practice following it in little things, then you will trust it in big things. I have a friend who is very intuitive. She sometimes calls up and says: "I've just had a hunch to call you up so I thought I would find out what it is about." Invariably I have some mission for her.

We are indeed living magic lives guided, protected, and provided for. All fear would be banished forever with a realization of this amazing system the Universal has provided for man. He would be unmoved by adverse appearances, knowing as the early Hebrews knew, "that Jehovah goes before, and every battle is won."

A friend told me a very interesting story. A man in the paper business in Kalamazoo, Michigan has given away a thousand of my books to his employees. He went into business on a small capital and gave up cold judgment and reasoning. He has built up a twelve-million-dollar business by following leads and hunches. All his workers have a knowledge of metaphysical law.

Another man who built his business upon the law of giving and receiving met with the same amazing success. He came to Philadelphia with a little money and bought a magazine, an old publication. His desire was to give the people a great deal for a very small price. He believed in the law of giving. It proved to be one of the most popular magazines. He gave the public the best in the way of stories and illustrations and paid well for them. The more he gave, the more he received millions poured in!! "Peace be within thy walls and prosperity within thy palaces!! Peace and prosperity go hand in hand. "Great peace have they that love Thy law, and nothing shall offend them." This law is the law of non- resistance. "Resist not evil, overcome evil with good." Transmute all failure into success, lack into plenty, and discord into peace.

CHAPTER 6.
Your Big Opportunity

You have only one judge, your word. Jesus Christ said, "I say unto you that every idle word those men shall speak, they shall give account thereof in the day of judgment, for by thy word thou shalt be justified, and by thy word thou shalt be condemned."

Every day is a day of Judgment. We used to be taught that it would be at the end of the world. Look back in your life and see how you have attracted either happiness or disaster through your words. The subconscious has no sense of humor. People joke destructively about themselves, and the subconscious takes it seriously. It is because the mental picture you make while speaking impresses the subconscious and works out on the external. A person who knows the power of the word becomes very careful of his conversation. He has only to watch the reaction of his words to know they do not return void. People make their worst mistakes by speaking while they are angry or resentful, because there is so much ill-feeling back of their words. Owing to the vibratory power of words, what you voice, you begin to attract. People who continually speak of disease, invariably attract disease.

Invisible forces are ever working for man, who is always pulling the strings himself, though he does not know it. We read in the Bible "Life and death are in the power of the tongue." Yet most people are speaking destructively from morning until night. It is because they have formed a habit of criticism, condemnation and complaint and are eager to tell you of their misfortunes and how mean all their relatives are. They wear their friends out and people avoid them. They are talking themselves into a flock of troubles. Now that we know the power of the word why not take advantage of it? We take advantage of the radio, the telephone and aero planes but live with the mound-builders in conversation.

Science and religion are now coming together. Science is discovering the power within the atom; metaphysics teaches the power within thoughts and words. We are dealing with dynamite when we deal with words. Think of the power of the word in healing! A word is spoken, and a chemical change takes place in the body.

One of my friends was seriously ill. The doctor said she had chronic bronchitis and was on the verge of pneumonia. Her daughters and the doctor rushed her to bed, and she had a nurse, but weeks passed and there was no improvement. She was a Truth student but for over a year had attended no meetings nor had she kept up her reading. One morning she telephoned me and said, "Please speak the word and get me out of this! I can't stand it anymore; I'm not sick, I'm just disgusted. So much negative talk and thought have almost floored me." Through the spoken word and her affirmation of Truth immediately there was a change for the better. She had a strong hunch to go out and was told it would be dangerous but by this time she was following Divine Guidance. She went out and called on me and said she was going to attend a luncheon the next day. What had happened? The words of Truth were making a change in her mind and a chemical change was taking place in her body. We are told that if we believe, never doubting, we can say to that mountain, "Be thou removed," and it would disappear into the sea.

The inexhaustible energy in man is released by good-will. A man free from fear, undisturbed by appearances, sending good-will to men and nations, could say to these mountains of hate and war; "Be thou removed" and they would return to their native nothingness.

Resentment and intolerance rob man of his power. We should have signs in the subways and shops "Watch your thoughts!" "Watch your words!"

Let us now be careful in directing this dynamic force within us. Let us direct it to heal, bless and prosper and direct it in waves of good to the whole world. It goes out a mighty force, but noiseless! Thought, the strongest power in the Universe is without sound. Your good-will sweeps all obstacles from your pathway and your heart's desire is released for you.

What is really yours? The answer is: "All that the kingdom affords is yours." Every righteous desire of the heart is promised you. There are three thousand promises in the Bible, but these gifts can come to us only if we can believe them possible, for everything comes through you, not to you. All life is vibration. Feel rich and you attract riches. Feel successful and you become successful.

I knew of a small boy who was born in a little country town with no advantages, but he always felt successful; he had the conviction that when he grew up, he would be a big artist. No one could discourage him because he was success; he had only success thoughts; he radiated success. At an early age he left the small town and went to a big city and to support himself he got a position as a newspaper artist on a daily paper, all this without previous preparation. It never occurred to him that it could not be done. He went to an art school and immediately became a shining light. He never studied in an academic way. Whatever he once saw he remembered. In a few years he went to a still larger city and became a well-known artist. This success came to him because he was always seeing success. "I will give to you the land that thou seeth."

The children of Israel were told that they could have all the land that they could see. The Bible is a metaphysical book, and it is speaking to the individual. This minute, it says to each one of us, "I will give to you the land that thou seeth." So, what are you seeing with your inner eye? What pictures are you inviting into your life? The imaging faculty has been called the scissors of the mind. If you have failure thoughts, reverse the thought with a success thought. This sounds easy enough to do, but when a failure thought has become a habit, it takes eternal vigilance to dislodge it. That is when a powerful affirmation is needed. You cannot always control your thought, but you can control your word, and eventually the word impresses the subconscious and wins out.

If you are in a negative state of mind, just take the statement: "I look with wonder at that which is before me!" It creates an expectancy of something wonderful and something wonderful will come to you. Cultivate the feeling that miracles and wonders are coming to pass. Cultivate a success expectancy.

Very few people bring into life what is rightfully theirs. They live on the outskirts of their heart's desire. It always seems too good to be true. To the person spiritually awake nothing is too good to be true.

If you want to hear people talking who are still asleep in the Adamic dream, go to a hairdresser's establishment. The Adamic dream is the illusion of opposites. Adam fell into a deep sleep having eaten of the tree of illusion. Of course, Adam stands for generic man the race-man. The race-man vainly imagined loss, lack, failure, sin, sickness, and death. The awakened man knows only one power, God, and one condition, good. But now we will return to the beauty parlor. The following is an exact quotation and a good example of what one hears: A woman sat down near me and said in a loud voice, "This place is too warm! Turn something on or open something." The attendant said to her, "How are you feeling today, Mrs. S?" She replied with a heavy sigh, "Oh, I'm pretty well, but I have a hard time keeping well." To the manicurist she said, "Why don't you wear glasses?" The girl replied,

"I don't need glasses, why should I wear them?" The woman replied, "Because everybody wears them. You'll find there is something wrong with your eyes if you have them examined." When she finally leaves, they all feel limp and wonder if they are really well or only seem to be well. She leaves a trail of apprehension and gloom. This is a sample of what one hears from nearly every booth; the way most people talk. It is appalling when one knows the power of the word and what they are attracting, for they are nearly all describing illnesses or operations.

You combine with what you notice so do not describe anything destructive for you begin to combine with it. What is really yours? The blessings you bring to yourself, through your spoken or silent word; the things you see with your inner eye. Only your doubts, fears and resentments keep your good from you. If you hate or resent a situation, you have fastened it to you, for you attract what you fear or dislike. For example: someone has been unjust to you, and you are filled with wrath and resentment. You cannot forgive that person. Time rolls on and another person does the same thing. It is because you have a picture of injustice engraved in your subconscious. History will repeat itself until you think you are cursed with misfortune and injustice. There is only one way to neutralize it. Be absolutely undisturbed by injustice and send good will to all concerned. "My good-will is a strong tower round about me. I now transmute all enemies into friends, all inharmony into harmony, all injustice into justice." You will be amazed at the working of the law. One student brought harmony out of chaos in her business affairs by that statement.

Do not look back and hash over hard times, or you will be drawn back into these conditions. Give thanks for the dawn of a new day. You must be immune to all discouragement and adverse appearances.

All that you desire or require is already on your pathway, but you must be wide awake to your good to bring it into manifestation. After making statements of Truth, you suddenly have a flash of realization. You suddenly feel yourself in a new environment. You feel old negative conditions falling away. I once said to a woman "The walls of lack and delay now crumble away, and you enter your promised land, under grace." She said she had a sudden flash of a wall crumbling away and that she stepped over it. Soon after that, the change came, and she really did enter her Promised Land of Plenty.

I knew a woman whose daughter's desire was a home and husband. In her early youth she had had a broken engagement. Whenever a possible marriage appeared on the horizon, she became frantic with fear and apprehension, picturing vividly another disappointment, and she had several. Her mother came to me to speak the word for her right marriage, divinely designed, which could not be interfered with. During the interview the mother said continually: "Poor Nellie! Poor Nellie!" I said: "Do not call your daughter 'poor Nellie' again. You are helping her to be demagnetized. Call her 'Lucky Nellie,' 'Fortunate Nellie, for you must have faith that God now gives to her the desires of her heart." The mother and daughter persisted in making their affirmations. She has now fulfilled her destiny for she is Mrs. Nellie, the demon of fear dissolved forever.

There are wonderful statements in the Bible referring to the breaking down of negative thought forms. "The power of the Spirit is mighty even unto the pulling down of strongholds." The human mind is helpless to cope with these negative thoughts. The victory is won by the God within, the superconscious mind.

"Brethren, whatsoever things are true, whatsoever things are honest, whatsoever things are just, whatsoever things are pure, whatsoever things are lovely, whatsoever things are of good report, if there be any virtue, and there be any praise, think on these things." Phil. 4: 8.

If people obeyed this, general conversation would come to a standstill for a while, until people learned to talk about constructive things.

CHAPTER 7.
In Nothing Be Anxious

All through the Bible we are told not to be anxious, not to be fearful, not to hoard or save, because an invincible, invisible power is at man's command to supply every need. But we were told that it would not work unless we believed in it. "If thou canst believe in this God Power, all things are then possible." It is difficult for man to believe in this power, because he has had a right training in unbelief. "I'll believe only what I can see," was supposed to be the height of wisdom. We lived in a world of externals, where we thought everything "just happened." We did not know that back of every happening was a cause, that we, ourselves, started in motion the machinery which produced good or evil in our pathway.

We did not know that words and thoughts are a form of dynamite, and should be handled carefully, with wisdom and understanding. We hurled out into the ethers, words of anger, resentment, or self-pity, then wondered why life was so hard.

Why not experiment with faith; trust this invisible God-Power and "In nothing be anxious," but "In everything by prayer and thanksgiving, let your requests be made known unto God." Could anything be more simple or direct? Anxiety and habit have become habits. The old thought-forms you have built up in the subconscious, hang on like barnacles on an ocean liner. But the ocean liner is put in drydock once in a while to have the barnacles scraped off, so, your mental barnacles will have to go through the same process. The drydock is a big situation.

I know of a woman who had been a coward all her life, particularly about finances. She worried all the time about money. She came into this Truth, realized how she had limited herself, and suddenly made the giant swing into faith. She commenced to trust God and not the external for her supply. She followed her intuitive leads about spending. If any of her clothes made her feel poor, she would discard them at once, getting something new to make her feel rich. She had very little money but gave one-tenth (a tithe) to good works. She was winding herself up into a new vibration. Very soon, things commenced to change on the external. A woman on whom she had no claim, who was merely an old friend of her family, left her a thousand dollars. A few months later, another thousand came in. Then a big door opened for her supply and many thousands came in. She had tapped her invisible supply from the Bank of the Universal. She had looked to God only for her supply, then the channels opened. The point I am bringing out is, that she had lost all anxiety about money matters. She had established in her subconscious, the firm conviction, that her supply came from God, and it never failed.

Man is an instrument for Infinite Intelligence to work through. It will express through him as success, happiness, abundance, health, and perfect self-expression, unless fear and anxiety make a short circuit.

If we want examples of fearless faith, go to the circus! The circus people perform seemingly impossible feats because they think they can and see themselves doing it. Faith means that you can see yourself receiving all these things that you desire. "I will give to thee the land that thou seest."

You can never do a thing you cannot see yourself doing or fill a place you cannot see yourself filling not visualizing, making, a mental picture (this is a mental process and often brings wrong and limited results), it must be a spiritual realization, a feeling that you are already there, be in its vibration.

I was very much impressed with the story of a great football player who was the greatest all-round athlete in the world, who trained in a hammock. One day he was lying there drowsing in the sun and the trainer came up to him with tears streaming down his face and said, "Jim, for the love of Mike and your country, won't you get up and out of that hammock and do something?" Jim opened one eye and said, "I was just thinking about that. I was going to send for you." "Good," said the trainer. "What do you want me to do?" "First," said Jim, "I want you to mark off twenty-five feet there on the ground." The trainer did so. "Then what?" said the trainer. "That's all," said Jim, and he closed his eyes and swung happily. After at least five minutes he opened them and looked at the marks for a few seconds and then closed his eyes again. "What's the idea?" yelled the trainer. "What are you doing?" Jim looked at him reproachfully and replied: "I'm practicing the broad jump." He did all his training in a hammock: seeing himself doing the broad jump.

Without the vision my people perish, in lack and limitation. You may work very hard on the external and accomplish nothing if you are without vision. Vision means to see clearly where you are going. To keep your eye on the goal. All men who have accomplished big things have done this.

James J. Hill, who built the Great Northern Railroad, said before a rail was laid, he heard with his inner ear the rumble of the trains and whistle of the engines. He had many obstacles to overcome, but his vision was so clear, it possessed him. One thing in his favor was that his wife believed in him. It is said that it takes two to make a dream come true.

Henry Ford, speaking of his mother-in-law said she was a fine woman, "She believed in me."

"When two of you agree, it shall be done." If you believe in yourself, others will believe in you. As you believe in yourself and the God-power within, fear and anxiety drop away. You establish the vibration of assurance. This is true of an intuitive person. Every move is made under Divine guidance, and he never violates a "hunch," therefore, he is always in his right place at the right time. However, it often takes great courage to follow intuition. It takes a Viking, who is unafraid, to sail in unknown seas. Claude Bragdon says: "To live intuitively is to live fourth-dimensionally." The magic path leads you out of the land of Egypt, out of the house of bondage. It is invaluable in business.

Never submit a hunch to someone on the reasoning plane. Those who have ears to hear, let them hear their intuitive leads, and give instant obedience.

"Whatsoever thou wilt ask of God, God will give it thee." This is true of each one. But if we have not received all the blessings of life, we have neglected to ask, or have not "asked aright." The Bible is teaching spiritual law and we must study and use it from every angle in order to set the great machinery of asking and receiving in motion. Every machine must be greased and oiled to be kept in good working order. Active faith and expectancy keep the machine of asking and receiving in perfect order. The following are some of the lubricants which keep it working. "When ye pray, believe ye have it." "In nothing be anxious." "Stand ye still and see the salvation of the Lord." "Do not limit the Holy One of Israel." Realization is manifestation.

Pray with praise and thanksgiving. Some people pray filled with anger and resentment. A woman wrote to me the other day saying: "I have just had a good talk with God, and I told Him just what He ought to do about it." She was in the habit of ordering people around and looked upon God as someone she could bully into doing something for her. God is the Supreme Intelligence within each one of us and we are the channels for It to express Itself. We must be non-resistant, poised, and peaceful, expecting our good to come to pass. We are the receivers, God is the Giver, and He must create His own channels. We find there is quite an art in praying aright. God must have right of way, His way, not your way. The moment you make your demand Infinite Intelligence knows the way of fulfillment. If you decide how your prayer shall be answered, you have blocked the divinely designed channel. Then you are apt to say: "I never have my prayers answered." We must acquire a technique and send out a sincere desire, which is a prayer. We are free from all clutch or anxiety when we say: "If this is according to the divine plan, we will receive it, if not, give us its equivalent." Be careful not to force anything not divinely planned.

We must know, that linked with God-power, nothing can defeat us. "God's ways are ingenious, His methods are sure."

Two of the most beautiful Psalms are the twenty-third and the one hundred and twenty-first. Both give one a feeling of absolute security and were written by a man who had experienced the working of spiritual law.

The God within protects, guides, and provides when fully trusted. Most people lose what they love most through fear of loss; they take every precaution on the external, not trusting the protection to the "Eye which watches over Israel." Put whatever you love under the law of divine protection.

The most important part of demonstrating is showing fearless faith. "I will go before thee and make the crooked places straight! I will break in pieces the gates of brass and cut in sunder the bars of iron." The Bible is talking about states of consciousness. "The gates of brass" and "bars of iron," are your doubts, fears, resentments, and anxieties. The gates of brass and bars of iron are of our own making and come from our own vain imaginings, a belief in evil.

There is a story of a herd of wild elephants: they were corralled in an enclosure, but the men had no way of keeping them in, so they dug stakes and put a rope all around the enclosure. The elephants thought they could not get out. They could have just walked over the rope and stepped out, but they had the illusion that the rope kept them in. This is the way with people: doubt and fear are a rope stretched around their consciousness. It makes it impossible for them to walk out into clear thinking.

Clear vision is like a man with a compass; he knows where he is going. Let intuition be your compass and it will always get you out of the woods. Even a man without a compass, led by intuition, would find his way out of the jungle, or be able to steer a ship at sea. Intuition will tell you to walk over the rope. It is amazing how people have overlooked their most important faculty intuition. Always on man's pathway is his message or lead. Often our leads seem trivial and silly. A person purely on the intellectual plane would dismiss them at once but the Truth student always has his spiritual ear to the spiritual ground, knowing he is receiving orders from the Infinite. The Bible speaks often of "the still small voice." It is a voice which is not an actual voice, though sometimes actual words are registered on the inner ear.

When we ask for guidance and lay aside the reasoning mind, we are tapping the Universal supply of all knowledge; anything necessary for you to know will be revealed to you. Some people are naturally intuitive and are always in contact with Universal Intelligence, but by taking an affirmation we make a conscious contact. Prayer is telephoning to God, and intuition is God telephoning to you. Many people have a "busy wire" when God telephones and they don't get the message. Your wire is "busy" when you are discouraged, angry or resentful. You've heard the expression "I was so mad I couldn't see straight." We might add, "I was so mad I couldn't hear straight." Your negative emotions drown out the voice of intuition.

When you are discouraged, angry, or resentful, is the time to make a statement of Truth, in order to get out of the woods of despair and limitation, for "Whosoever calleth on the name of the Lord shall be delivered!" There is a way out, "Reveal to me the way."

We must stop planning, plotting, and scheming and let Infinite Intelligence solve the problem in Its own way. God-power is subtle, silent, and irresistible. It levels mountains and fills in valleys and knows no defeat! Our part is to prepare for our blessings and follow our intuitive leads.

We now give Infinite Intelligence right-of-way.

CHAPTER 8.
Fearlessness

"Why are ye fearful, 0 ye of little faith?"

All through the Bible man is told not to be afraid. Fear is man's only enemy. It is faith turned upside down. Jesus Christ said, "Why are ye fearful, 0 ye of little faith?" If you can only believe, all things are possible. Linked with God-power, man is invincible. The story of Jehosophat is the story of the individual. So often he seems outnumbered by adverse appearances, but he hears the same voice of the Infinite saying: "Be not afraid or dismayed by reason of this great multitude, for the battle is not yours but God's." Jehosophat and his army were even told that they would not need to fight the battle. "Set yourselves, stand ye still and see the salvation of the Lord," for the battle was God's not theirs. Jehosophat appointed singers unto the Lord to praise the beauty of holiness as they went out before the army, saying; "Praise the Lord for His mercy endured forever." When they came toward the watchtower in the wilderness they looked toward the multitude and behold, they were dead. The enemy had destroyed itself. There was nothing to fight. The Bible is talking about states of consciousness. Your enemies are your doubts and fears, your criticisms, and your resentments. Every negative thought is an enemy. You may be outnumbered by adverse appearances but be not afraid or dismayed by reason of this great multitude; for the battle is not yours but God's.

As we follow closely the story of Jehosophat, we see he advanced making an affirmation: "Praise the Lord, His mercy endured forever." He had nothing to say about the enemy or his own lack of strength. He was giving the Lord his full attention, and when he commenced to sing and praise, the Lord placed ambushments against his enemies and they were smitten. When you make your statements of Truth your enemy thoughts are vanquished, dissolved, and dissipated, therefore, all adverse appearances disappear. When Jehosophat and his army came toward the watchtower in the wilderness, they looked into the multitude and behold they were dead. The watchtower in the wilderness is your high state of consciousness, your fearless faith, your place of safety. There you rise above all adverse conditions, and God's battle is won.

"When Jehosophat and his people came to take away the spoils of the enemy, they found among them both riches and precious jewels, more than they could carry away, and they were three days in gathering of the spoil, it was so much." That means, when you let God fight the battle for you, great blessings come out of every adverse situation. "For thy God will turn the curse into a blessing, for the Lord thy God loveth thee." The ingenuity of the Spirit is amazing. It is pure intelligence and brooks no interference with its plans. It is very difficult for the average person to "stand still," which means, keep your poise, and let Infinite Intelligence run the situation. People like to rush into the battle and try to manage things themselves, which brings defeat and failure.

"Ye shall not need to fight in this battle; set yourselves, stand ye still and see the salvation of the Lord with you. Tomorrow goes out against them, for the Lord will be with you." That means, not to run away from the situation, walk up fearlessly, and face the lion on your pathway, and the lion turns into an Airedale. The lion takes his fierceness from your fear. A great poet has said "Courage has genius, magic and power in it.

Daniel was unafraid and the lions' mouths were closed. King Darius called to Daniel while he was yet in the lions' den, asking him if God could save him from the lions, and Daniel answered, "0! King live forever! My God hath sent His angels and shut the lions' mouths that they have not hurt me." We have in this story the subdued attitude of the lions as a result of Spiritual power; the entire group changed from ferocity to docility, and Daniel looking away from the beasts to the Light and Might of Spirit, which saved him completely from the lions. Scarcely a day passes without some sort of lion appearing on man's pathway, the lions of lack, limitation, fear, injustice, dread, or forebodings. Immediately walk up to the situation of which you are afraid. If you run away from it, it will always be right at your heels.

Many people lose the things they prize or love because they are continually fearing their loss. They do everything possible on the external to ensure protection, but back of it all is the devastating picture of fear. In order to hold the things, you prize and love, you must know that they are Divinely protected, therefore, nothing can harm them. I give the example of a woman who was very fond of a man who was good-looking and popular with women. She decided to prevent his meeting one particular woman of her acquaintance because she was sure the woman would make every effort to "cut her out," to use a slang expression. One evening she went to the theatre and there he was with the woman. They had met at a card party. Her fears had actually attracted the situation. I knew a woman who had seven children. She knew they were all Divinely protected, and they all grew up safe and sound. One day a neighbor rushed in and said, "You had better call your children, they are all climbing up and down trees, they are going to kill themselves!" My friend replied, "0 they're only playing tree-tag. Don't look at them and nothing will happen." Like Daniel, she turned her back to the situation and let God take care of it.

The average person is a resenter, a resister, or a regretter. They resent people they know and people they don't know. They resist everything from daylight saving up. They regret what they did or what they didn't do. It is very wearing to be with these people. They exhaust all their friends. It is because they are not living in the wonderful NOW and are losing all the tricks in the game of life.

It is heaven to be unafraid and to live fully in the now that is to be fearless in using what we have, knowing back of us is the abundance of the spheres to draw upon. We know that fearless faith and the spoken word release this supply. The power of the word was known in Egypt thousands of years ago.

We read in the Bible, "Behold I make all things new!" By our words of truth, we can make new our minds, bodies, and affairs. When all fear is obliterated, we live magic lives. Like Jehosophat we go forward fearlessly singing: "Praise the Lord, His mercy endured forever." In our watchtower of high consciousness, we stand still and see the salvation of the Lord.

Christianity is founded on faith. Faith gives one a sublime assurance of one's good. One may be surrounded by adverse appearances, but this sublime assurance impresses the subconscious mind, and a way opens for the manifestation of health, wealth, and happiness. There is an endless, invisible supply for every man. "Before we called, we were answered." This supply is waiting to be released by faith and the spoken word. We find that Jesus Christ taught an exact science.

At the World's Fair there was a panorama of New York City in the Edison Building. At dusk when the city was being lighted up the buildings showed a myriad of lights; the man explaining the exhibit said: "The city is lighted by the power of electricity at the turn of a switch, the turn of a hand." Edison was the man who had faith in the laws of electricity. He knew what could be done with it if it were harnessed and directed. It seemed to have intelligence of its own. He created a dynamo through which it would work, after years of patience and loving absorption in his work. Now this power lights the world, for it is harnessed and directed.

Jesus Christ taught man to harness and direct thought. He knew that fear was as dangerous as uncontrolled electrical forces. Words and thoughts must be handled with wisdom and understanding. The imagination is man's workshop, and an imagination running wild and building up fear pictures, is just about as safe as riding a bucking broncho.

We were born and brought up in an age of doubt and fear. We were told that the age of miracles was over and to expect the worst. An optimistic person was laughed at. A bright remark was,

"A pessimist is a person who lives with an optimist." "Eat the speckled apples first," was thought the height of wisdom. They did not seem to realize that by following this advice they would never catch up with the good apples, for they would be speckled too by the time they were reached.

What a beautiful world this would be if all anxiety and fear were blotted out. These twins, anxiety, and worry have made men slaves and are destroyers of health, wealth, and happiness.

There is only one way of getting rid of fear and that is, to transmute it into faith; for fear is the opposite of faith. "Why are ye fearful, 0 ye of little faith?" These words ring down through the centuries. Jesus Christ taught that the Father within man could be absolutely trusted to guide, protect, and provide when man believes it possible. Jesus Christ demonstrated this God-power over and over again in order to convince his followers. Out of the invisible supply He brought the loaves and fishes; He raised the dead; and took money from the fishes' mouths. He told them, "Greater things shall ye do, for I am going."

We know he was teaching an exact science, the science of mind, the power of thought and the power of the word. We must have faith, for faith registers the idea in the subconscious mind. When an idea is once registered in the subconscious, it must objectify. That is the reason Jesus Christ told people that if they believed (which is having faith), all things were possible. How are we to get rid of this anxiety, which we might call "anti-faith"? The only way to neutralize it is to walk up to the thing you are afraid of.

There was a man who had lost all his money. He was living in very poor quarters and all the people around him were poor and he was afraid to spend the little he had. All he had was about five dollars. He had tried to get work, but everyone had turned him down. He awoke one morning to face another day of lack and disappointment, when the idea (or hunch) came to him to go to the horse show. It took about all he had but he was fired with the idea of being with rich and successful people again. He was tired of his limited surroundings. He fearlessly spent the money for a ticket to the Horse Show. There he met an old friend, who said: "Hello Jim,! Where have you been all this time?" Before the Show was over the old friend gave him a wonderful position in his firm. His hunch and fearless attitude toward money had put him in a new vibration of success.

Form the habit of making giant swings into faith. You will receive marvelous returns.

As has already been noted, we look with amazement at the people in the circus performing their remarkable feats. These people have the faith that they can perform these acts and see themselves doing them. You cannot accomplish anything you cannot see yourself accomplishing. These difficult feats are all a matter of poise and balance. Your success and happiness depend upon your poise and balance. Trusting God is like walking a slack wire. Doubt and fear cause you to lose your balance and fall off into lack and limitation. Like the circus performer, it takes practice. No matter how many times you fail, try it again. Soon you will acquire the habit of poise and balance. Then the world is yours. You will walk joyfully into your kingdom. The circus performers all seem to love their work, no matter how difficult. The band plays, the people applaud, and they smile, but remember they were trained without the music and applause.

Rhythm, harmony, and balance are the keys to success and happiness. When you are out of rhythm you are out of luck.

In the fourth chapter of Philippians, we read: "Be careful (or anxious) for nothing; but in everything by prayer and supplications, with thanksgiving, let your requests be made known unto God." This is certainly a wonderful arrangement, all in favor of man. Man, free from worry and fear, asks with thanksgiving, and his good is given him.

CHAPTER 9.
Victory And Fulfillment

Victory and fulfillment are two wonderful words and since we realize that words and thoughts are a form of radio activity, we carefully choose the words we wish to see crystallized.

Life is a crossword puzzle; the right word gives you the answer. Many people are rattling off destructive words in their conversation. We hear them say: I'm broke! I'm sick! Remember by your words you are justified and by your words you are condemned. You are condemned by them because they do not return void. Change your words and you change your world, for your word is your world. You choose your food, and the world is now calorie conscious. People no longer eat buckwheat cakes, beefsteak, potatoes, pie and three cups of coffee for breakfast. To keep down weight they eat dry toast and orange juice. This is tremendous discipline, but they are working for results. Why not try a diet of the right words for you are literally eating your words. That is the value of the affirmation. You are deliberately building up a constructive idea in your consciousness. Your consciousness may be crammed and jammed with destructive ideas, but continually making a statement of Truth, will dissolve these negative thought-forms. These thought- forms have been built up from your own vain imaginings. Perhaps as a child you were taught that life was hard, happiness fleeting, and that the world was cold and unfriendly. These ideas were impressed upon your subconscious, and you found things just as they were predicted. With a knowledge of Truth all these external pictures may be changed, for they are only pictures, which change as your subconscious beliefs change.

When I tell people about the power of the word, and those words and thoughts are a form of radio activity and do not return void, they say: "Oh, is it as easy as that?" Many people like things difficult and hard to understand. I believe that was the reason the amazingly simple teachings of Jesus Christ were forgotten after a few hundred years. People build up creeds and ceremonies which they only half understand. Now, in this twentieth century, the secret things are being revealed and we are again having primitive Christianity.

"Ask, believing, thou shalt receive!" We know that our beliefs or expectancies are impressed upon the subconscious and carried out. We might say, if you ask, not believing, you will not receive. Faith creates expectancy.

This Infinite Intelligence upon which man draws his supply is called, by Jesus Christ, "Your Heavenly Father." The Father within, He described as a kind, loving parent desirous of pouring all good things upon His children. "Fear not, little flock, 'tis your Father's good pleasure to give you the Kingdom." He taught that God's law was simply a law of love and good-will. "Love your neighbor as yourself' "Do unto others as you would be done by." Any violation of the law of love causes a short circuit. "The way of the transgressor is hard." God is immutable law "I am the Lord (law), I change not."

Divine ideas are immutable, not subject to change. What wonderful Words, "Immutable not subject to change."

A woman came to me filled with fears and forebodings. She said for years she had been pursued by the fear that even if she should receive the desire of her heart, something would happen to spoil it. I gave her the statement: "The Divine Plan of your life is a perfect idea in Divine Mind, incorruptible and indestructible, and cannot be spoiled in any way." A great load was lifted from her consciousness. For the first time in years, she had a feeling of joy and freedom. Know the Truth and the Truth gives you a sense of freedom, soon then comes the actual freedom on the external.

This Supreme Intelligence is what man becomes one with when he speaks the word. This Supreme Intelligence awaits man's direction, but it must have right of way, it must not be limited.

Divine Activity in your body brings health. There is only one disease congestion and one cure circulation. Congestion and stagnation are the same thing. People say they "have got into a rut." A new idea will take them out of a rut. We must get out of the rut of negative thinking.

The word enthusiasm in the dictionary is defined, "to be inspired or possessed by a god." Enthusiasm is divine fire and kindles enthusiasm in others. To be a good salesman you must be enthusiastic about the articles you are selling. If you are bored with your business or uninterested, the fires go out, and no one else will be interested.

A woman came to me for success in business. She said, "I have a shop, but it is usually empty. I do not bother to open it until late in the day, what's the use?" I replied, "There is indeed no use so long as you feel the way you do. You are keeping people away. Become enthusiastic over what you have to sell. Be enthusiastic about yourself. Be enthusiastic about the God-power within you and get up early to open your shop and be ready for the big crowd."

By this time, she was all wound up with divine expectancy. She dashed down to her shop as early as possible, and people were waiting outside and poured in all day.

People often say to me, "Treat my business." I say, "No, I will treat you, for YOU are your business." Your quality of thought penetrates every article for sale and all the conditions connected with it. Jesus Christ was divinely enthusiastic about the message He had to bring to the

Father within each man. He was enthusiastic about faith. He told the people that whatsoever they "ask in His name" would be given them. It was a message of asking and receiving. He told them just how to comply with spiritual law. "Ask, believing, thou shalt receive." "When ye pray believe ye have it." "Why are ye fearful, oh, ye of little faith?"

After two thousand years His divine fire is rekindled in the consciousness of all Truth students. We are having a Christian renaissance, a new birth, a revival of Christianity. He taught a universal principle, without creed or ceremony. We see members of all religions, denominations, coming into this Truth movement. It does not take them away from their churches. In fact, many clergymen are now teaching what the metaphysicians are teaching; for Jesus Christ is the greatest of all metaphysicians, because He proved His principles and brought miracles to pass. He sent forth His disciples, "To preach the Gospel and heal the sick." For about three hundred years His message survived, then his divine fire was lost and the words, "Be thou healed," were no longer spoken. Creed and ceremony took their place. Now we see people flocking to these Truth Centre's to be healed, blessed, and prospered. They have learned to "Pray aright," and have understanding faith.

A woman told me of an answered prayer. Her son wrote her that he was going to southern California on a business trip in his car. She read in the morning paper of a flood, and she immediately spoke the word for divine protection. She had a great feeling of security she knew he would be protected. She soon heard from him, saying some business had interfered with his leaving, so he was detained. If he had left when he had expected, he would have been in the flood district.

We become divinely enthusiastic about our answered prayers, which we call "demonstrations," for it means that we have demonstrated the truth and have been set free from some limitation.

The 24th Psalm is one of the most enthusiastic of the many Psalms of praise and thanksgiving.

"Lift up your heads, oh ye gates and be ye lifted up ye everlasting doors; and the King of Glory shall come in. Who is this King of glory, the Lord strong and mighty, the Lord mighty in battle."

The gates and doors symbolize man's consciousness. As you are lifted up in consciousness, you contact the super-conscious, the God within, and the King of glory comes in. This King of glory lifts your burdens and fights your battles, solves your problems.

The average person has a difficult time letting the King of glory come in. Doubt, fear, and apprehension keep the doors and gates locked against your good.

A student told me of a situation which she attracted by negative thinking. She had been invited to a gathering of old and valued friends. It was of the utmost importance for her to be there. She was so anxious to go, she said to herself repeatedly, "Oh, I hope nothing happens to interfere." The day of the reception arrived, and she awoke with a terrific headache. At one time she had been subject to these headaches, going to bed for several days, but she had not had one for many years. Her doubts and fears had attracted this disappointment. She called me up and said, "Will you please speak the word that I will be well by evening to go to the reception?" I replied, "Why, of course, nothing can interfere with God's perfect plan." So, I spoke the word. Later, she told me of her miracle. She said in spite of the way she felt, she prepared to go. She cleaned her jewelry, got her dress ready to wear, and attended to every detail, though she felt scarcely able to move. Very late in the afternoon, she said she had a peculiar sensation as of a fog lifting in her consciousness, and she was perfectly well. She went to the reception and had a wonderful time. I believe that the healing might have come more quickly had she not said, "I want to be well by tonight." We are continually limiting ourselves by our words, so not until night was, she perfectly well. "By your word you are justified and by your word you are condemned."

I knew a man who was the Centre of attraction wherever he went, because he was always enthusiastic about something. Whether it was about shoes, clothes, or a haircut, he enthused others into buying the same things. He did not gain anything material by it, he was just naturally enthusiastic. Someone has said, "If you want to be interesting to others, be interested in something." An interested person is an enthusiastic person. We often hear people say: "Do tell me what you're interested in."

Many people are without vital interests and are hungry to hear what other people are doing. They are usually the ones who keep the radio turned on from early morning till late at night. They must be entertained every minute. Their own affairs do not hold enough interest.

A woman once said to me: "I love other people's affairs." She lived on gossip. Her conversation consisted of, "I was told," "I was given to understand," or "I heard." It is needless to say she is now paying her Karmic debt. A great unhappiness has overtaken her, and everyone knows about her affairs. It is dangerous to neglect your own affairs and to take an idle curiosity in what others are doing. We should all be busily engaged in perfecting ourselves but take a kindly interest in others. Make the most of your disappointments by transmuting them into happy surprises. Transmute all failure into success. Transmute all unforgiveness into forgiveness, all injustice into justice. You will be kept busy enough perfecting your own life, you won't have time to run other people's affairs.

Jesus Christ aroused the enthusiasm of the multitudes by performing miracles, healing the sick and raising the dead. "And a great multitude followed Him because they saw His miracles which He did for them that were diseased." As we read this, we feel the enthusiasm of the multitudes, which surrounded Him. With Him all things were possible, for He knew that He and the Father were, indeed, one.

With divine enthusiasm I bless what I have and look with wonder at their increase.

LIST OF TITLES WITH ISBN NO.

ISBN	TITLE
9788194914129	1984
9789390575220	1984 & Animal Farm (2In1)
9789390575572	1984 & Animal Farm (2In1): The International Best-Selling Classics
9789390575848	35 Sonnets
9789390575329	A Clergyman's Daughter
9789390575923	A Study In Scarlet
9789390896097	A Tale Of Two Cities
9789390896837	Abide in Christ
9789390896202	Abraham Lincoln
9789390896912	Absolute Surrender
9789390896608	African American Classic Collection
9789390575305	Aldous Huxley: The Collected Works
9789390896141	An Autobiography of M. K. Gandhi
9789390575886	Animal Farm
9789390575619	Animal Farm & The Great Gatsby (2In1)
9789390575626	Animal Farm & We
9789390896158	Anna Karenina
9789390575534	Antic Hay
9789390896165	Antony & Cleopatra
9789390896172	As I Lay Dying
9789390896226	As You like it
9789390575671	At Your Command
9789390575350	Awakened Imagination
9789390575114	Be What You Wish
9789390896233	Believe In yourself
9789390896998	Best of Charles Darwin: The Origin of Species & Autobiography
9789390896684	Best Of Horror : Dracula And Frankenstein
9789390575503	Best Of Mark Twain (The Adventures of Tom Sawyer AND The Adventures of Huckleberry Finn)
9789390896769	Black History Collection
9789390575756	Brave New World, Animal Farm & 1984 (3in1)

9789390896240	Brother Karamzov
9789390575053	Bulleh Shah Poetry
9789390575725	Burmese Days
9789390896257	Bushido
9789390896066	Can't Hurt Me
9788194914112	Chanakya Neeti: With The Complete Sutras
9789390896042	Crime and Punishment
9789390575527	Crome Yellow
9789390575046	Down and Out in Paris and London
9789390896844	Dracula
9789390575442	Emersons Essays: The Complete First & Second Series (Self-Reliance & Other Essays)
9789390575749	Emma
9789390575817	Essential Tozer Collection - The Pursuit of God & The Purpose of Man
9789390896578	Fascism What It Is and How to Fight It
9789390575688	Feeling is the Secret
9789390575190	Five Lessons
9789390575954	Frankenstein
9789390575237	Franz Kafka: Collected Works
9789390575282	Franz Kafka: Short Stories
9789390575060	George Orwell Collected Works
9789390575077	George Orwell Essays
9789390575213	George Orwell Poems
9788194914150	Greatest Poetry Ever Written Vol 1
9788194914143	Greatest Poetry Ever Written Vol 1
9789390896301	Gulliver's Travel
9789390575961	Gunaho Ka Devta
9789390575893	H. P. Lovecraft Selected Stories Vol 1
9789390575978	H. P. Lovecraft Selected Stories Vol 2
9789390896059	Hamlet
9789390575022	His Last Bow: Some Reminiscences of Sherlock Holmes
9789390896134	History of Western Philosophy
9789390575121	Homage To Catalonia

9789390896219	How to develop self-confidence and Improve public Speaking
9789390896295	How to enjoy your life and your Job
9789390575633	How to own your own mind
9789390896318	How to read Human Nature
9789390896325	How to sell your way through the life
9789390896370	How to use the laws of mind
9789390896387	How to use the power of prayer
9789390896028	How to win friends & Influence People
9788194824176	How To Win Friends and Influence People
9789390896103	Humility The Beauty of Holiness
9789390896653	Imperialism the Highest Stage of Capitalism
9789390575084	In Our Time
9789390575169	In Our Time & Three Stories and Ten poems
9789390575145	James Allen: The Collected Works
9789390896189	Jesus Himself
9789390575480	Jo's Boys
9789390896394	Julius Caesar
9789390575404	Keep the Aspidistra Flying
9789390896400	Kidnapped
9789390896424	King Lear
9789390575824	Lady Susan
9789390896455	Law of Success
9789390896264	Lincoln The Unknown
9789390575565	Little Men
9789390575640	Little Women
9788194914174	Lost Horizon
9789390896462	Macbeth
9789390896929	Man Eaters of Kumaon
9789390896523	Man The Dwelling Place of God
9789390896349	Man The Dwelling Place of God
9789390575909	Mansfield Park
9788194914136	Manto Ki 25 Sarvshreshth Kahaniya
9789390896509	Marxism, Anarchism, Communism
9789390575664	Mathematical Principles of Natural Philosophy

9788194914198	Meditations
9789390575800	Mein Kampf
9789390575794	Memory How To Develop, Train, And Use It
9789390896486	Mind Power
9789390896585	Money
9789390575039	Mortal Coils
9789390575770	My Life and Work
9789390896035	Narrative of the Life of Frederick Douglass
9789390575152	Neville Goddard: The Collected Works
9789390575985	Northanger Abbey
9789390896530	Notes From Underground
9789390896547	Oliver Twist
9789390575459	On War
9789390575541	One, None and a Hundred Thousand
9789390896554	Othelo
9789390575435	Out Of This World
9789390575015	Persuasion
9789390575510	Prayer The Art Of Believing
9789390575091	Pride and Prejudice
9789390896561	Psychic Perception
9789390575381	Rabindranath Tagore - 5 Best Short Stories Vol 2
9789390575367	Rabindranath Tagore - Short Stories (Masters Collections Including The Childs Return)
9789390575374	Rabindranath Tagore 5 Best Short Stories Vol 1 (Including The Childs Return
9789390896622	Romeo & Juliet
9789390896127	Sanatana Dharma
9789390575596	Seedtime & Harvest
9789390896639	Selected Stories of Guy De Maupassant
9789390575206	Self-Reliance & Other Essays
9789390575176	Sense and Sensibility
9789390575299	Shyamchi Aai
9789390896738	Socialism Utopian and Scientific
9789390896646	Success Through a Positive Mental Attitude
9789390575428	The Adventures of Huckleberry Finn

9789390575183	The Adventures of Sherlock Holmes
9789390575343	The Adventures of Tom Sawyer
9789390896691	The Alchemy Of Happiness
9789390575862	The Art Of Public Speaking
9789390896288	The Autobiography Of Charles Darwin
9788194914181	The Best of Franz Kafka: The Metamorphosis & The Trial
9789390575008	The Call Of Cthulhu and Other Weird Tales
9789390575107	The Case-Book of Sherlock Holmes
9789390896110	The Castle Of Otranto
9789390896745	The Communist Manifesto
9789390575589	The Complete Fiction of H. P. Lovecraft
9789390575497	The Complete Works of Florence Scovel Shinn
9789390896820	The Conquest of Breard
9789390896813	The Diary of a Young Girl
9789390896332	The Diary of a Young Girl The Definitive Edition of the Worlds Most Famous Diary
9789390575701	The Great Gatsby, Animal Farm & 1984 (3In1)
9789390575312	The Greatest Works Of George Orwell (5 Books) Including 1984 & Non-Fiction
9789390575992	The Hound of Baskervilles
9789390896707	The Idiot
9789390896714	The Invisible Man
9789390575657	The Knowledge of the holy
9789390575558	The Law & the Promise
9789390896721	The Law Of Attraction
9789390896776	The Leader in you
9789390896363	The Life of Christ
9789390896196	The Man-Eating Leopard of Rudraprayag
9789390896783	The Master Key to Riches
9789390575268	The Memoirs Of Sherlock Holmes
9789390896479	The Midsummer Night's Dream
9789390575466	The Mill On The Floss
9789390896790	The Miracles of your mind
9789390896660	The Mutual Aid A Factor in Evolution
9789390896448	The Origin of Species

9789390896905	The Peter Kropotkin Anthology The Conquest of Bread & Mutual Aid A Factor of Evolution
9789390896806	The Picture of Dorian Gray
9789390896271	The Picture of Dorian Gray
9789390575275	The Power Of Awareness
9789390896356	The Power of Concentration
9788194824169	The Power of Positive Thinking
9789390575411	The Power of the Spoken Word
9788194914105	The Power Of Your Subconscious Mind
9789390896899	The Power of Your Subconscious Mind
9789390896417	The Principles of Communism
9789390575787	The Psychology Of Mans Possible Evolution
9789390896615	The Psychology of Salesmanship
9789390575732	The Pursuit of God
9789390575398	The Pursuit of Happiness
9789390896851	The Quick and Easy Way to effective Speaking
9789390575947	The Return Of Sherlock Holmes
9789390575138	The Road To Wigan Pier
9789390896981	The Root of the Righteous
9789390575855	The Science Of Being Well
9788194914167	The Science Of Getting Rich, The Science Of Being Great & The Science Of Being Well (3In1)
9789390896011	The Screwtape Letters
9789390896073	The Screwtape Letters
9789390575336	The Secret Door to Success
9789390575695	The Secret Of Imagining
9789390896868	The Secret Of Success
9789390896431	The Seven Last Words
9789390575930	The Sign of the Four
9789390896004	The Sonnets
9789390896516	The Souls of Black Folk
9789390896875	The Sound and The Fury
9789390575244	The State and Revolution
9789390896882	The Story of My Life
9789390896936	The Story Of Oriental Philosophy

9789390896752	The Strange Case of Dr. Jekyll and Mr. Hyde
9789390896943	The Tempest
9789390575916	The Valley Of Fear
9789390575879	The Wind in the willows
9789390896080	The Wind in the willows
9789390575763	Their eyes were watching gofd
9789390575831	Three Stories
9789390896950	Twelfth Night
9789390896592	Twelve Years a Slave
9789390896677	Up from Slavery
9789390896974	Value Price and Profit
9789390896967	Wake Up and Live
9789390896493	With Christ in the School of Prayer
9789390575602	Your Faith is Your Fortune
9789390575473	Your Infinite Power To Be Rich
9789390575251	Your Word is Your Wand
9789390575718	Youth
9789391316099	A Christmas Carol
9789391316105	A Doll's House
9789391316501	A Passage to India
9789391316709	A Portrait of the Artist as a Young Man
9789391316112	A Tale of Two Cities
9789391316747	A Tear and a Smile
9789391316167	Agnes Gray
9789391316174	Alice's Adventures in Wonderland
9789391316136	Anandamath
9789391316181	Anne Of Green Gables
9789391316754	Anthem
9789391316198	Around The World in 80 Days
9789391316013	As A Man Thinketh
9789391316242	Autobiography of a Yogi
9789391316266	Beyond Good and Evil
9789391316761	Bleak House
9789391316778	Chitra, a Play in One Act
9789391316310	David Copperfield

9789391316075	Demian
9789391316785	Dubliners
9789391316051	Favourite Tales from the Arabian Nights
9789391316235	Gitanjali
9789391316068	Gravity
9789391316150	Great Speeches of Abraham Lincoln
9789391316662	Guerilla Warfare
9789391316839	Kim
9789391316822	Mother
9789391316211	My Childhood
9789391316846	Nationalism
9789391316327	Oliver Twist
9789391316853	Pygmalion
9789391316334	Relativity: The Special and the General Theory
9789391316389	Scientific Healing Affirmation
9789391316341	Sons and Lovers
9789391316587	Tales from India
9789391316372	Tess of The D'Urbervilles
9789391316396	The Awakening and Selected Stories
9789391316402	The Bhagvad Gita
9789391316303	The Book of Enoch
9789391316228	The Canterville Ghost
9789391316907	The Dynamic Laws of Prosperity
9789391316006	The Great Gatsby
9789391316860	The Hungry Stones and Other Stories
9789391316433	The Idiot
9789391316440	The Importance of Being Earnest
9789391316297	The Light of Asia
9789391316914	The Madman His Parables and Poems
9789391316457	The Odyssey
9789391316921	The Picture of Dorian Gray
9789391316464	The Prince
9789391316938	The Prophet
9789391316945	The Republic
9789391316518	The Scarlet Letter

9789391316143	The Seven Laws of Teaching
9789391316525	The Story of My Experiments with Truth
9789391316532	The Tales of the Mother Goose
9789391316549	The Thirty Nine Steps
9789391316594	The Time Machine
9789391316600	The Turn of the Screw
9789391316983	The Upanishads
9789391316617	The Yellow Wallpaper
9789391316426	The Yoga Sutras of Patanjali
9789391316990	Ulysses
9789391316624	Utopia
9789391316679	Vanity Fair
9789391316020	What Is To Be Done
9789391316686	Within A Budding Grove
9789391316693	Women in Love

www.ingramcontent.com/pod-product-compliance
Lightning Source LLC
LaVergne TN
LVHW090937230826
846093LV00009BA/417

* 9 7 8 8 1 9 5 9 6 1 7 3 3 *